Pamphlet Architecture 28

Augmented Landscapes

Smout Allen

Princeton Architectural Press, New York

Published by
Princeton Architectural Press
37 East Seventh Street
New York, New York 10003

Visit our web site at www.papress.com.

This project is supported in part by an award from the National Endowment for the Arts.

NATIONAL
ENDOWMENT
FOR THE ARTS

Editor: Scott Tennent
Design: Smout Allen

Special thanks to: Nettie Aljian, Sara Bader, Dorothy Ball, Nicola Bednarek, Janet Behning, Megan Carey, Becca Casbon, Penny (Yuen Pik) Chu, Russell Fernandez, Pete Fitzpatrick, Sara Hart, Jan Haux, Clare Jacobson, John King, Mark Lamster, Nancy Eklund Later, Linda Lee, Katharine Myers, Lauren Nelson Packard, Jennifer Thompson, Paul Wagner, Joseph Weston, and Deb Wood of Princeton Architectural Press
—Kevin C. Lippert, publisher

Library of Congress Cataloging-in-Publication Data

Smout, Mark.

Augmented landscapes / Mark Smout, Laura Allen, Neil Spiller.
80 p. : chiefly ill. ; 22 cm. — (Pamphlet architecture ; no. 28)

ISBN-13: 978-1-56898-625-8 (alk. paper)
ISBN-10: 1-56898-625-4 (alk. paper)

1. Landscape architecture. I. Allen, Laura, 1969– II. Spiller, Neil. III. Title. IV. Series.

SB469.37.S66 2007
712—dc22

2006029366

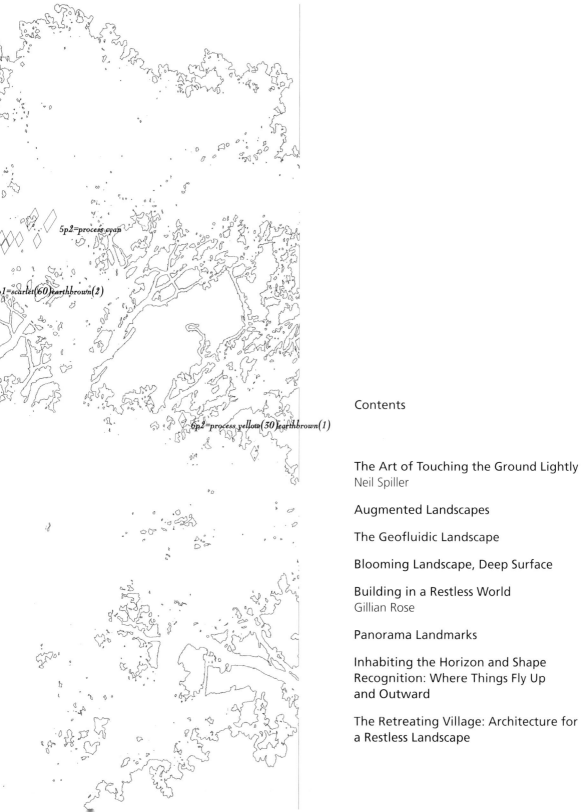

5p2=process cyan

1=scarlet(60)earthbrown(2)

6p2=process yellow(30)earthbrown(1)

Contents

The Art of Touching the Ground Lightly
Neil Spiller

Augmented Landscapes

The Geofluidic Landscape

Blooming Landscape, Deep Surface

Building in a Restless World
Gillian Rose

Panorama Landmarks

Inhabiting the Horizon and Shape
Recognition: Where Things Fly Up
and Outward

The Retreating Village: Architecture for
a Restless Landscape

The Art of Touching the Ground Lightly
Neil Spiller

At the outset it must be said that it is an honor to be asked to write this introduction to the work of my friends Laura Allen and Mark Smout. Most times of the day or night they are in their studio, positing, honing, and creating architecture of astounding dexterity, subtleness, and minimal ecological disruption. This they do with the happy humor of people really enjoying the intimacy of working together and the strange dance of fecund creative activity.

But we are getting ahead of ourselves; can we search back in their pasts to ascertain an architectural lineage? Laura Allen was once a student of Peter Cook. Mark Smout was once a student of Christine Hawley, Nat Chard, and CJ Lim; indeed Smout was at the helm of some of Lim's most notable projects of the 1990s. They both tutor as well as having studied at the Bartlett. Their teaching unit is highly regarded and often is rewarded with medals from the Royal Institute of British Architects. Like any teachers of architecture worth their salt, generations of students have acted as guinea pigs for their ideas. But never does a student ever match that Smout Allen light touch or indeed that Smout Allen directness of approach, a stripping away of all that is superfluous, gratuitous, and fetishized.

So what is, as we architectural alchemists say, the prima materia of their work? Firstly the siting of their work is never random and never expedient; it is always vastly important and is the fundamental generator to the project. Much inspiration is gleaned from geomorphic natural phenomena. Architectural objects make up multi-scaled machinic ecologies, both within individual buildings and between groups of buildings. There is a healthy interest in the machine: painting machines, crossbows, computers, and the crazy graphic machines of Heath Robinson, though Robinson's English garden shed aesthetic of twine and walking-stick never manifests itself in their work. They must design finely articulated armatures, and very beautiful they can be.

Their work is always attuned to issues of time, duration, weather, and weathering. The work rejoices in the dusk, the sunset, and the horizon—the changing position of the viewer, the user, and the idle observer all carefully choreographed and accommodated. Nor are they ones to avoid a full understanding of the flora and fauna of their sites. They may introduce more vegetal variety into the sites and use the byproducts of their growth to drive other aspects of the building. Their work is modern without being stupidly avant-garde; it speaks of a quieter, more assured understanding of genius loci. In fact the Smout Allen world is one of tracking and instigating loci to architectural effect. It is indeed of its own time.

If perhaps there is one other architect I am reminded of when viewing Smout Allen architecture, it is surely Peter Salter, a quintessentially English architect of a generation or two before them. Their work has many of his qualities; it is very different in form, yet shares a formidable interest in detail used to create a contemporary organic architecture that juxtaposes and finely joins materials. Both architects share a kind of Voyseyian crafted concern for sumptuousness. But unlike Salter, Smout Allen is also cosseting the virtual in some of their work. This is not embedded in the work with the usual fanfare and light show but in a simple and pragmatic way that further enhances their dioramas and set pieces.

Another distinguishing aspect of Smout Allen's production is their use and expertise in graphics. All good architectural designers should experiment with the various modes of representation open to them, but Smout Allen are virtuosi of techniques. They sketch like a dream, but when these sketches evolve into presentation drawings they take on an almost religious intensity. The first thing that must be said about these drawings is how *clean* they are. Blimey they are clean! These marks must have been drawn by hands wearing snooker referee's gloves. Not for them the grungy patina of a well-worked working drawing or the grubby paw print and greasy splodge.

The quality of lines on the drawings is very pure, no jolt and no fade. The drawings themselves are composed with protocols which abound with a type of contemporary cubist minimalism, each view on top of one other. It is through these drawings that the genetics of each scheme is revealed to us as a series of spatial relationships at once teased and delightfully manicured.

Smout Allen is a delightful young practice. They are harbingers of a new architecture. An architecture that touches the land lightly because nothing else seems appropriate anymore. An architecture that forsakes the meaningless pyrotechnics of our current generation of technocratic architects yet uses technology appropriately and sensitively. Enjoy the joy.

Neil Spiller is Professor of Architecture and Digital Theory at The Bartlett School of Architecture, UCL.

Augmented Landscapes
Smout Allen

Onokami Village, Gunma Prefecture, Toshio Shibata, 1994. Japan's land retention structures exquisitely tailor concrete and geotextiles to the ground surface.

Restless Landscapes

Man continues to mark the land, relentlessly shaping the surface from wilderness to cultivation. Strategies of mechanization, the necessity of irrigation, and the demands of inhabitation introduce a new order. So the "countryside," which has evolved over centuries, can be described as under the influence of nature but under the control of man. The "natural" landscape has taken on an artificial patination. Alien materials interrupt the processes of growth and decay. New and evolving features created by man are, to an extent, absorbed by the fluid and yielding nature of our surroundings. What results is a hybrid environment, a utilitarian topography, a sustained artifice.

Oxford Tire Pile No. 8, Westley, California, 1999. Edward Burtynsky's photographs demonstrate an edgy relationship between nature and technology. The reshaping of terrain by modern industrial activities of refineries, quarries, and waste sites, often photographed at indeterminate scale, illustrates the vast extent of man's intervention in the landscape. The result is an appreciation of the built environment as "man-made sublime."

This neo-nature has become a picturesque aesthetic, an often cherished rural environment where sentimental attitudes that inform our visual perception of the landscape become key. Representations of the landscape play an important role in our understanding of our environment. The picturesque parkscapes and paintings of the eighteenth century enabled the viewer to appreciate from a distinct distant position an idealized rural scene. In the nineteenth century panorama and diorama theaters were a popular attraction in major cities. The panoramas represented the desire to discover and understand the horizon in the perceptual world. This developed the use of perspective and spatial depth in constructing an image of a view. The panorama was a viewing mechanism that taught people how to see a view as it organized the visual experience for the eye.[1] Vistas depicting urban and rural landscapes were skillfully painted in such a realistic way that visitors were convinced that they were at the scene. The illusion was often enhanced by the use of real objects positioned with perspectival accuracy in the foreground. These painted scenes are an expression of landscape as both a visualization of "natural" space and as a spectacle.

Jørgen Dehs describes the current acknowledgment of the word "landscape" as not simply a geographical term but as a metaphor:

We have an interest in landscape when we feel the need to stretch our eyes. Along with this common understanding—and probably because of it—the term

Houses on Dauphin Island, Alabama, have evolved stilts to rise above the surf of the hurricane and flood–prone Gulf Coast.

landscape enjoys a comprehensive career as a metaphor.... Every chaotic totality is assembled into a unity as soon as it is labelled a landscape. The term "urban landscape" sheds a redeeming glow upon even the most dejected neighbourhood; "industrial landscape" transforms any romping ground for the ravages of industry into an object of aesthetic sensibility.[2]

In this Pamphlet we discuss five design cases. In each the physicality of site and the processes of environmental transformation are exploited—the intrinsic features of the landscape, the force of nature, geography, climate, geology, and land use are all scrutinized. The resulting architectural interventions respond to their dynamic and fluxing territories. The ephemeral character of the environment is reflected in the solidity of the artifacts that inhabit it as they take on a local specificity and lend to their surroundings a sense of nature illuminated.

Restless Drawings
Each design case expresses a unique response to the augmentation of architecture and its prevailing relationship to the restless landscape. In addition, hand in hand with notions for architectural space, materiality, and program, observational and representational concepts are used through which the mutability of nature can be exposed. The role of "making"

in the design process includes documentary photography, collages, prototypes, models, and drawings, which work as two- and three-dimensional examinations of site, behavior, and events, rather than purely representing notions of static space and material. Normative demonstrations of architectural space by means of orthographic projection are avoided, as these tend to depict simplified, flattened or foreshortened viewpoints. The creation of test sites on and in the surface of the paper allows the work to react to and describe the iterative process of design. This work becomes a materialization of the practice of design.

Scale and Superfluity
As a consequence of subtle investigations of site that pick up on ephemeral conditions as diverse as the hue of the sunset reflected on wet ground or the discovery of subterranean medieval field patterns, the work holds within it an intensity and abundance of information. Modeling and drawing methods enable this detail to become apparent. For example, the Grand Egyptian Museum vitrine (pages 14–21) does not attempt to emulate the desert topography; instead it is conceived as a rock pool with a defining surface under which, on close inspection, there is a colorful and rich diversity of life. The Panorama Landmarks (pages 26–43), although of a similar scale are not scaled in a traditional sense; each is

The Claude Glass, or Landscape Glass, became a popular accessory for tourists and amateur painters of the eighteenth century who toured the "picturesque" landscape for inspiration and enlightenment.

designed to be held in the palm of the hand or explored by being held up to the sky. This enables them to be viewed at the scale of an object or within the scale of the horizon.

Scope and Scape

The "scope" of landscape—the careful view or examination—and the "scape"—the expansive scene—provide a duality that is employed by the architecture and experienced by its occupants. This relationship can be considered as the "miniature" to the "gigantic" as defined by the cultural theorist Susan Stewart:

> Our most fundamental relation to the gigantic is articulated in our relation to landscape, our immediate and lived relation to nature as it "surrounds" us…. We move through the landscape; it does not move through us. This relation to the landscape is expressed most often through an abstract projection of the body upon the natural world. Consequently, both the miniature and the gigantic may be described through metaphors of containment—the miniature as contained, the gigantic as the container. [3]

The Claude Glass, a notable example of a tool devised in the pursuit of the understanding of landscape, was a device by which one could visibly reduce the large expanse of landscape into a framed composition.

A more contemporary example of a technique by which to contrive a composition is the matte paintings of the movie industry, now sadly redundant. These were used to augment reality by adding or subtracting from the scene. Unlike the Claude Glass, careful positioning is crucial to enable the desired single and static views to be directly related to the panoramic scenes.

Each Panorama Landmark takes up its position in the anatomy of its surroundings. The viewer is precisely placed relative to the horizon on which new elements are positioned, juxtaposed to the fore-, mid-, and background. The drawings for the Retreating Village (pages 55–79) are typically made on flat sheets. However, in the endeavor to realize both the scope and scape of the landscape, to depict time and duration, and the dynamism of their disintegrating territory, they exist between the realm of sketch diagrams and architectural orthographic representations. They contain multiple viewpoints and simultaneous shifts of position.

Mutability

We have used kinetic models and devices to illustrate the restlessness of the environment or the trajectory of the architecture. These provide one with numerous ways with which to contemplate the work. In addition, the viewer is permitted a greater intimacy with the

Irrigation produces verdancy in the arid desert.

project, becoming a participant. Daguerre's back-lit diorama paintings of the 1820s are a recurring reference. They mastered a subtle yet impressive technique that revealed, as a theatrical display, the transition of dawn or dusk over the chosen scene by a simple adjustment of relative light levels across and behind the canvas.

The notion of exposure has a direct influence on the Horizon Projects (pages 44–51). Each Light-Box is constructed with layers of translucency and color. They are viewed against a variable "sky" of light that reveals the shape, shine, shadow, and silhouette of objects held in their horizon. The Ballistic Devices are deployed instantly and appear only fleetingly on the horizon. They provide a momentary examination of space.

Merry-go-round landscape from the filming of *Annie Get Your Gun* (1950) gave the background landscape the illusion of movement as if viewed from a train.

Environmental Technologies

The projects described here develop technological strategies in a manner that fuses them into the body of the architecture. These technologies are essentially environmental as they employ air, water, sun, and earth to augment the performance of the building as well as the landscape; modifying open and exterior spaces at the same time as enclosures. The technology is embedded, contextual, and visual.

The Grand Egyptian Museum celebrates the vernacular technologies of arid and semi-arid countries, which are used to substantially moderate the environmental comfort of the galleries. However, these can be reinterpreted for subtle and unexpected effects. The Geofluidic Landscape's (pages 10–13) intricate play of rock and water is activated to shift and displace elements of the architecture. The technological interface—the materiality between the building and the landscape, is a conspicuous relationship. The architecture is dramatized by the performance of the landscape.

The Geofluidic Landscape

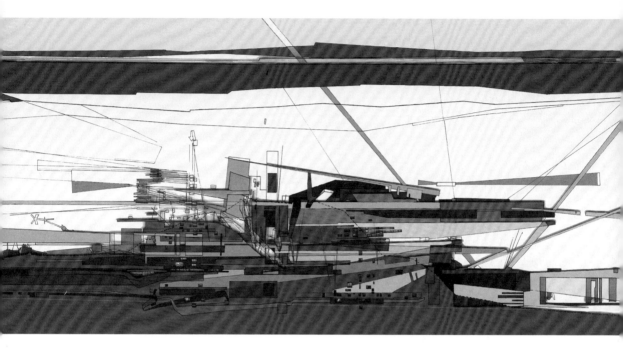

The site on Nessodden Peninsula in Southern Norway has a spectacular 300-degree view of the horizon. The rock is a literal edge between the sea and the land, and the building that inhabits it merges and blurs the boundary so that in essence the architecture becomes part of the geological and topographical landscape.

The passage of abundant water on the site provides a source of kinetic energy that invades the building. Trenches, gullies, and reservoirs are cut into the rock to channel water throughout the gardens and through the service core. Counterbalances and weights shift building pieces. The internal space and the external form are reconfigured, as the floors become walls, panels move to reveal new spaces, and garden beds are raised and tilted toward the sun. The water flow also provides the energy to power the building.

Illuminating the Coastal Facade: The Geofluidic Landscape is represented in a painting made up of three layers that reveal the building's relation to the landscape from real to abstract. The top layer abstracts time sequences and space. Light highlights the building facade.

This moving landscape requires complex control. A "computer" and its processors take the form of fluidic switches within the rock landscape at a super-enlarged scale—large enough to be viewed at a distance. The computer's decision-making processes are therefore made physical. For example, its inputs, logic gates, and outputs become fountains, flows, small pools, and jets so that the complex choreography of the landscape, building, and fluidic devices perform in a reciprocal although not repetitive sequence. The rock landscape is sculpted by water channels and fountains and is veiled by sprays and steam.

See-Thru Rock Landscape: The bottom layer
continues to depict light paths but rationalizes the
landscape by detailing the rock troughs and fluidic
switches. The algae–growing bags (on the right),
compost hoppers (on the left), fountains, jets, and
fluidic switches are shown in greater detail.

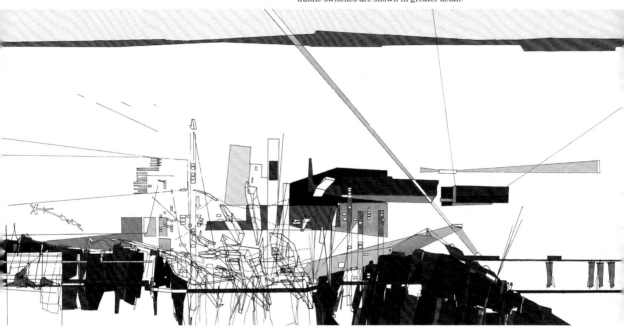

The building provides a suitable environment for growth, divided into two gardens. On the first, produce is grown on a raised landscape of allotments that employ both natural and controlled environments relating to sub-arctic gardening. The second garden is an artificial environment growing algae for fish food, suspended in vertical sacks. This is propagated by intense artificial light. The "light box" intentionally spills light north, directly back to Oslo, and south, creating fluctuating shards of light that fall across the buildings.

The building explores the natural cycles and processes that are present in the surrounding landscape and apparent in the ambient and latent qualities of the site. Diurnal light, tidal flow, texture, color, etc., are highlighted and accentuated. One is introduced to these phenomena with heightened sensitivity by means of tranquil areas such as hot pools, viewpoints, and sun-drenched plateaus.

From both land and sea the building and gardens can be seen as sequences of horizontal stripes formed by the kitchen, breakfast bar, and garden plate. This horizontal banding is illuminated by intense artificial light flickering across the facade. The visual dashes are countered by both horizontal and vertical dots formed by lifts and the passage of the trolleys around the site. The dots and dashes have varying pace and diagrammatically suggest the level and specifics of occupation. The coastal facade is perceived from a greater distance and as such the visual indicators are at a greater scale and a slower pace. This facade comprises markets, tranquil areas, a summer restaurant, and alfresco areas, all of which are seasonally "shut down" and folded away.

Plan at +1.5 meters:
A: Main water pipe
B: Rock trough
C: Rock piton
D: Trolley counterweight
E: Fluidic processor cut into rock
F: Deceleration bag
G: High-pressure hoses

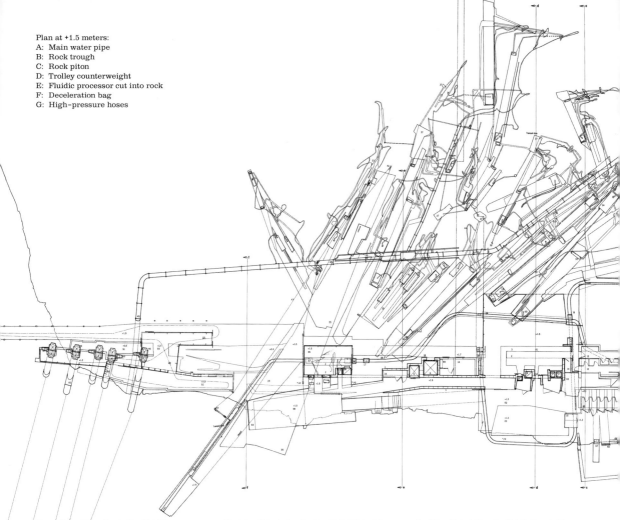

Prevention of Freezing in the Fluid Lines
An obvious problem with an external fluid system
in a cold climate is freezing. The high freezing point
of water and the low temperatures of the sub-arctic
winter mean that measures will have to be taken to
prevent freezing, bursting, and irreparable damage.

Heat-loss Calculation for the High Pressure Hoses
Assuming 14 devices with 60m
per device = 840m of pipe
Pipe internal diameter (ID) 200mm with 100mm of
insulation

A = 1,057.4m^2
therefore
U = 0.018 + 3
  = 3.18
to be kept at +10°C at -10°C
Hl = 3.18 x 1,057.4 x 20 = 67,251W
the total consumption at -10°C is
67,251 + 6,471 + 2,740 = 76,462W, or 76kW

Heat-loss Calculation for the Main Water Pipe
Assuming 110 meters of pipe, pipe ID is 800mm
with 200mm insulation, to be maintained at
constant 10°C.

Heatloss = overall resistivity x area x °C
Hl = $UA (T_1-T_2)$
Area = πDL
where D = diameter and L = length
A = 3.147 x 1.2m x 110
A = 415.4m^2
U = 0.18 surface resistivity with
  0.03 W/m of standard insulation
therefore
0.03
0.2 (thickness of insulation) = 0.15W/k
U = 0.18 + 0.15
  = 0.33
Hl = $UA (T_1-T_2)$
to be kept at +10°C at -10°C
Hl = 137 (-10-10) = 2,740W

Heat-loss Calculation for Fluidic Supply Pipes
Assuming 14 devices @ 60m of pipe per device
  = 840m of pipe in total
Pipe ID is 60mm with 60mm insulation.
A = 475.8m^2
therefore
U = 0.18 + 0.5
  = 0.68
to be kept at +10°C at -10°C
Hl = 0.68 x 475.8 x 20 = 6,471W

Providing Power for Heating the Pipes
It can be shown that the maximum power
demand of 176kW, in a worst–case scenario,
can be achieved using hydropower.

In the proposal, the penstock enters the turbines
at just above sea level. The turbines convert the
potential energy of the water from the Semsvannet
reservoir on the west side of the fjord.

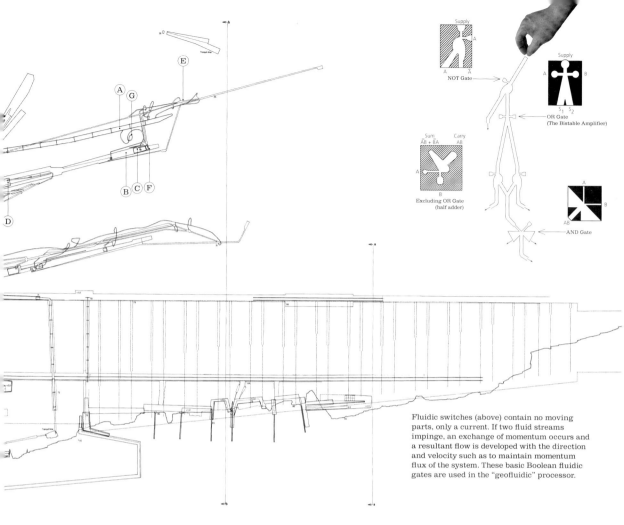

Fluidic switches (above) contain no moving parts, only a current. If two fluid streams impinge, an exchange of momentum occurs and a resultant flow is developed with the direction and velocity such as to maintain momentum flux of the system. These basic Boolean fluidic gates are used in the "geofluidic" processor.

Activating the Rock Troughs and Fluidic Switches

The spatial "shut down" of semi-permanent areas is achieved by a simple mechanical system of pulleys and armatures (attached to the building), and counterweights and brakes that are anchored in the rock landscape.

Calculation of Head Requirement to "Float" a Rock Piton

A rock weighing 16kN needs to be balanced by the head of water. To find the theoretical mass, at which a pipe with ID 900mm can float, the volume of the pipe must first be determined.

$$\text{volume} = \pi.r^2.\text{length}$$
$$= 0.63m^2(145m)$$
$$= 91.35m^3$$

with water having $10kN/m^3$
$$\text{force} = 913kN$$
with granite having $20kN/m^3$
$$m^3 = 45.6m^3$$

This means that the head of water in the specified pipe could theoretically "float" $45.6m^3$ of granite. This is ample for the proposal.

Friction Calculation for Moving the Rock Piton

Load and mass required to "hold" a lift by means of a rock piton, when the lift car weighs 2kN. A safety factor of four is applied, giving the weight of the lift as 8kN.

The assumed friction coefficient of the rock, as a brittle solid:

μ	= 0.5
F	= μW
8kN	= 0.5 (W)
W	= 16kN

Granite weighs $20kN/m^3$, therefore:

rock	= $0.8m^3$

A granite rock of $0.8m^3$ on a flat surface of granite will resist a force, in this case the 8kN lift car. The force required to move the rock when it is "floating" on water is:

μ	= 0.01
F	= 0.01(16,000)
F	= 160N

Calculation for the Volume of the Water Trolley

Known quantities are:
  2kN of lift car (full)
  160N to move floating rock piton
  20 degree incline for trolley

assumed:
  10% loss of power in mechanism

trolley unloaded is balanced with lift unloaded.

Therefore the total force required to move the
  device   = 2,376N

As the trolley is on an incline,
  force:load = height:length
  2,376:load = 1:5
  trolley load required   =11,880N, or 12kN

water at $10kN/m^3$ a volume =$1.2m^3$

This is the maximum volume of water required in the trolley to pull a full lift car to the top of the building.

Blooming Landscape, Deep Surface

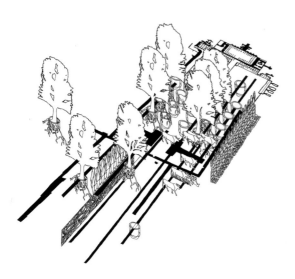

Left: Diagrammatic arrangement of structures, water, and planting based on the plan and painted reliefs of incense trees and cattle from the funerary temple of Queen Hatshepsut at Deir el-Bahari.

Water was a fundamental feature in ancient Egyptian garden design. Canals cut into the gardens fed water into the orchards and planting beds. Trees were planted in pits cut into the ground of inner gardens so they could each be watered. Water for refreshment was provided in pools. To aid access, these had stepped edges that were revealed as the water level dropped.

The site for the Grand Egyptian Museum is manipulated as conceptual archeology. A "deep surface" is laid into the desert geology, puncturing, excavating, and compressing the ground around vast galleries for the museum's collection of Egyptian antiquities. The three subterranean galleries are connected by chasms for ventilation, circulation, and division of the collection. The landscape skin and roof structures are merged into stratified layers and interstitial spaces laid down to combat the extremes of the local environment. These are carefully configured with zones of bright sun and deep shade, interspersed with draught corridors and plenum spaces. Roof structures, which peel up from the ground, generate locally accelerated wind flow and evaporative cooling.

The design responds to Egypt's indigenous landscape and its traditions. Ancient Egyptian gardens created synthesis between building and landscape using changes in levels, terraces, and viewpoints. Gardens were plotted with trees, groves, and pools in symmetrical arrangements. Environmental modification was achieved with unroofed inner courtyards and sunken atrium gardens shaded with tree canopies and vine pergolas. The augmented landscape—a blooming and watery condition—is in living and verdant contrast to the desert. The museum's vast roofscape is flooded with water; irrigation channels for the roof plate "fields" fray into the surrounding dunes, occasionally allowing sunlight to filter through them to the museums below. The water drains to a shallow delta which is planted with indigenous flora, acting as a vegetal chronograph of diurnal and seasonal abundance. These wells produce a caustic light that drenches the walls and floor of the galleries.

The museum is also adorned to take advantage of the passage of the sun across the site. The chasms are clad in faience tiles, a glazed material that replicated the effect of precious blue-green stones. The Egyptians called it *tjehnet*, meaning "that which is brilliant," and its surface gleams and glistens with a light that became a metaphor for life and eternity. The tiles are faceted to reveal an array of shadows and shimmering reflections at dawn, noon, and dusk.

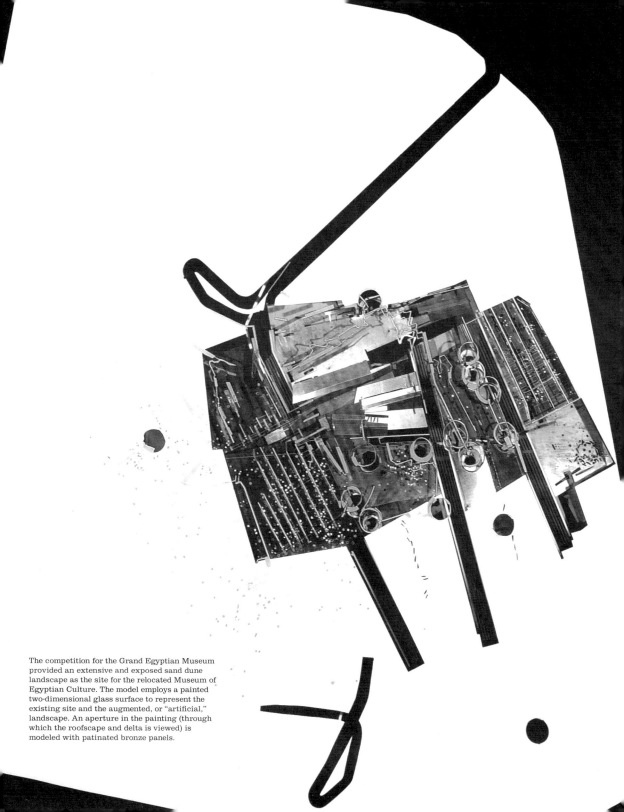

The competition for the Grand Egyptian Museum
provided an extensive and exposed sand dune
landscape as the site for the relocated Museum of
Egyptian Culture. The model employs a painted
two-dimensional glass surface to represent the
existing site and the augmented, or "artificial,"
landscape. An aperture in the painting (through
which the roofscape and delta is viewed) is
modeled with patinated bronze panels.

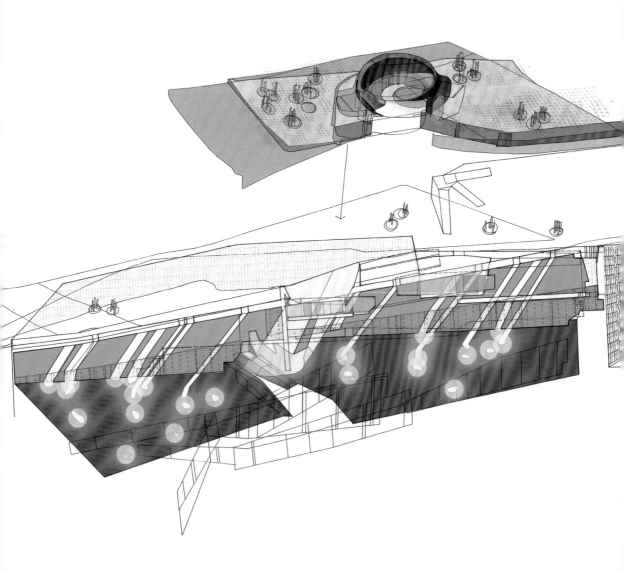

Section through the museum galleries,
auditorium, and service spaces shows the
"deep surface" penetrated by light via cuts in
the irrigated plate and through the sunken
workshops suspended above the museum floor.

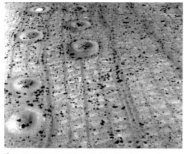

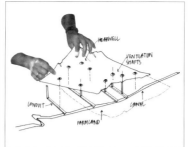

Qanats are an ancient water-management system typical in desert regions that allow large quantities of water from underground aquifers to be delivered to the surface without the need for pumping, exploiting ground water as a natural resource. The surface is pockmarked by vertical shafts that lift cooled air from the *qanat* tunnels to the surface, cooling the air above ground.

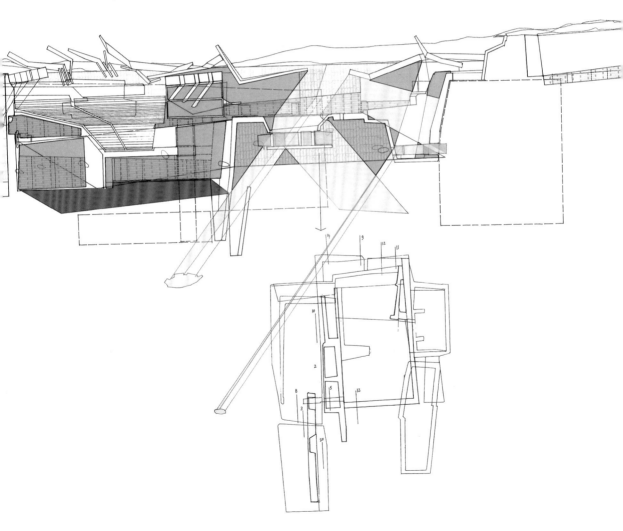

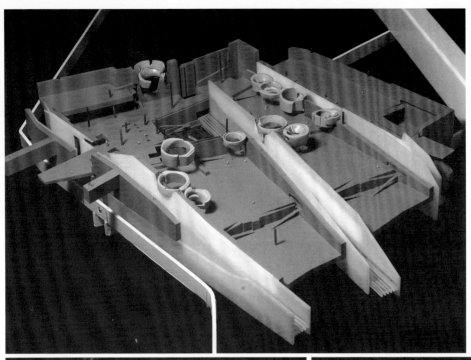

Left: Model with augmented landscape removed. The main galleries are exposed below the skin. Eleven sunken workshops are suspended in the "deep surface."

Below: The landscape plates, roofs, and gardens contribute to the museum's environmental strategy.

Right: Diagram of the museum's technical performance.

A: Chasms (external public areas) chronographically regulate light and shade

B: Tiled linings to chasm walls. Faceted tiles have a partial faience face to reflect the midday sun. Unfinished matt facets absorb and diffuse solar energy at dawn and dusk.

C: Excavated "deep surface" gallery spaces and circulation

D: Water-chilled draught corridors and service tunnels

E: The vegetal chronograph, a diurnally and seasonally changing landscape of blossoming vernacular planting. Varieties of water lilies bloom throughout the day, the blue from morning to midday and the white from late afternoon to the following day.

F: Final stages of the far-reaching *qanat* network. Networks of this kind bring life to an otherwise uninhabitable desert.

G: Cisterns

H: Irrigated "flood plain" gardens

I: Sunken and shaded workshop courtyards pierce and puncture the augmented landscape.

J: Evaporative cooling from irrigated landscape to museum spaces below (the Ancient Egyptians hung wet mats outside as cooling devices).

K: Mass temperature is controlled by constantly regulating the flow of water in the irrigated landscape and therefore the overflow of water down the chasm faces and floors.

L: Profiled roof surfaces, with "wet blankets" to the internal faces, provide ventilation of thermally modified air to the main body of the museum.

M: Horizon

N: A frayed edge exists between the natural dunescape and the augmented landscape.

O: Prevailing wind draws out the museum's stale air through profiled surfaces.

P: Surface perforations

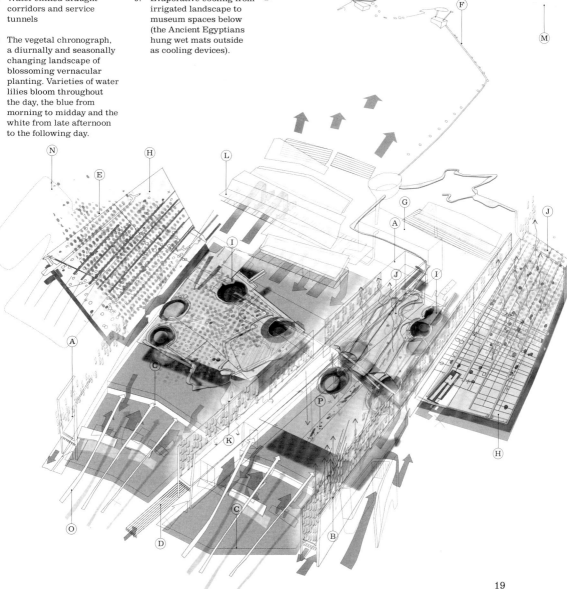

The augmented landscape

Building a Restless World
Gillian Rose

It has been the case for some time now that the work of making interventions in the world has to conceive of itself as precisely that: intervening in a world. Our sense of place has gone global. So interventions have to happen not in the local, or at least not only in that, but in a world stretched out and strung around, a world patched together by a wide range of differentiated, variable, and erratic processes in which the human and the non-human are hard to distinguish. More people are pushed and pulled into being on the move than ever before; viruses mutate and global pandemics threaten; the worldwide web provides shelter for a proliferation of voices and images; neoliberal economic policies meet resistance of all kinds; climate change offers both devastation and new ecological niches; violence proliferates and a new generation of commentators have been both horrified and thrilled by what they can see of how the world has globalized.

For many, this extraordinary globalizing has been met with an excitable, not to say hyperbolic, response. Mike Davis hails ecological disaster, Jean Baudrillard sees a world swallowed by simulacra, Frederic Jameson frames globalization as the shadow play of the late capitalist economy, Paul Virilio plunges into its speed and militarization. We are dazzled by its information and image overload, which according to Guy Debord is nothing other than our own alienation. Time and space are both compressed in distracting ways, according to David Harvey. The dizzying rush of this world has no use for monuments, apparently, other than those celebrating the economic and political arrangements of this new world order. The durability of monuments from before this world came into being can only invoke irony and hauntings in these transforming times. Rather, the world is now spectacularized. It appears that Hollywood blockbusters and contemporary artists are best placed to diagnose our condition, and we move between the multiplex and the art gallery when we want to find the world reflected.

But it seems that my own writing here has been seduced by the rhetoric it refers to, and I need to be more careful. In taking more care, it is also necessary to avoid positing an alternative to this vision of global madness which is simply its flipside: an equally promiscuous myth of utopic stasis, where all is local, time stands still, and conflict is unknown. This utopia is sought in any number of places and in any number of ways. Sometimes it is imagined in cities, dreamt of as cosmopolitan places where differences mingle convivially. Sometimes it takes the form of national imagined communities, with boundaries holding fast against immigrants, refugees, viruses, ideas. But most often, this safe place is imagined as rural. Raymond

Williams, among others, has traced the emergence and durability of this peculiarly English dream of the countryside as a stable, traditional place where nothing much changes except the seasons. It is a dream that increasing numbers of Brits are attempting to realize abroad rather than at home, but this is only testimony to its enduring seductiveness: the countryside imagined as a garden, enclosed, nurtured and nurturing. Of course, this dream of unchanging tranquility is as much a fantasy as its dystopic inverse, with its urbanized scenario of doom and revenge.

Because, of course, everything is on the move, everything is changing, and much of it always has been. Mobility and dynamism are the norm, and they always have been. The questions this prompts are: What is on the move? How? Why? And with what effects? What sort of geographical imagination can help us engage in this world? We are used to maps of the world, to globes, to photographs of the Earth from space. They all offer versions of the world as a plane. All that there is can be located on a two-dimensional grid: everything has a place and only one place; no two things can be in the same place. This vision of the world was slowly pieced together as it was explored and annexed by mostly colonizing Europeans between the sixteenth and eighteenth centuries. It is a modern vision of the world, in which all is

visible, knowable, categorizable—as well as one that erased all signs of its own violent and mobile production. But it is also a vision of the world that arguably no longer holds, or at least only holds in quite local circumstances. That European hegemony over global mapping has been fundamentally challenged. The geographical imaginations we need now to understand something of how the world is globalized are much more nuanced and less straightforward. There are no all-enveloping planes any more. Rather, we need more elaborate spatial vocabularies to describe the many registers and modalities through which globalizing processes are at work.

For example, some aspects of globalization might best be indicated by putting the terms *flow* and *territory* together. Some kinds of globalizing mobilities might best be thought of as flows, when things physically move from one place to another and their path, even if convoluted or mediated, can somehow be mapped. Flows of people, commodities, carbon, and capital trace intricate global cartographies. So too do birds, seeds, and viruses. And so too do continents in their grand drifts around the world (although they "drift" only in geological time; in our historical time, their convulsive jerks are much more violent and disruptive). Flows also congeal, though they run in particular patterns, are halted at certain boundaries, and are orchestrated from specific, bounded locations (flows of international capital, for example, depend on the social arrangements of very particular places for their mobility: the financial districts of certain world cities and offshore tax havens). Particular places will show their own specific symptoms of this dynamism which changes their geography, as flows impinge on what felt like more or less stable territories or disrupt yet again territories that felt like they should be stable.

Indeed stability might best be sought in a place-specific sense of rhythmic change, rather than in a denial of change through dreams of static and enclosed places. Richard Mabey has argued this, in his account of becoming well again by experiencing (and writing about) a change of location and the seasons of the year in that new place.[4] The seasons, indeed the days and minutes, carried the dynamism of that new place, as plants shooted, blossomed, and died back, as migrant animals came and went, and as his house responded to heat, wet, cold, and wind. Mabey's account of becoming well also offers another argument. As he listens, looks, and thinks about his embeddness in the world, Mabey suggests that a sensitivity to the environment needs nurturing and is not antithetical to analysis and representation. Indeed, he suggests that mediated responses to the non-human world are an essential part of being human. There is a need, he says, for a mediated responsiveness to the flows and territories of our globalized world. Mediation gives us pause as well as pleasure, perhaps, or discomfort. Mediation's hesitations are necessary interruptions in our relation with worldly things. Those mediations might take the form of a diary, a house, an artist, or a memory—or kites, ducting systems, platform emplacements, or a camera obscura. Pausing over these things to reflect on those relations can perhaps help us to think beyond the two responses to globalization with which this essay began. We do not have to be overwhelmed by its force, nor do we necessarily need to seek refuge in naïve relations with where and who we are. Being invited to think about the relations we have with the world is a moment in which those relations might change, however fleetingly.

Then there are those other geographies. Not of flow and the territories they interrupt, but of distances and the proximities that striate them. These can also be the geographies of conventional discussions of globalization: alliances between those distant in physical terms but brought together by political struggle, for example, or the emotional closeness of families scattered by migration, or the cultural negotiations of diasporic identities. But these geographies can also be more surprising. A flash of vivid memory interrupting a news report; a ghostly sighting; a persistently awkward place; a photo that won't go away; a sense of loss or surfeit; a half-remembered caress. Strange, passing, and not always predictable, these moments can also come at us from outside. A flash of light, an unexpected reflection. A wall of light baffles, the unnecessary beauty of frozen water, the pleasures of sand and wind, a kite playing with the wind. Being disturbed by such surprises may not always be pleasurable, of course, just as moments of reflection on relations with the world may not be. But it does seem that they are as much part of this world we inhabit as are the more evident flows in which we are entangled. They might act as reminders of that entanglement. Interventions into that world then, if they wish to settle however temporarily, would do well to evoke them too.

The interplay of territory with flow, and proximity with distance, are some of the geographies that speak to current processes of globalization. They suggest that interventions into that world thus globalized should engage with those geographies if they are to be effective. Landscapes are on the move all around us, and so too are their unexpected excesses. Interventions that play with both of these are likely to be those that resonate most in the contemporary world.

Gillian Rose is Professor of Cultural Geography at The Open University.

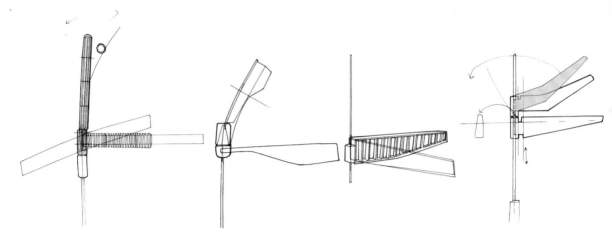

Sketches showing the articulation of the glinting
limbs of "drift markers" placed out to sea.

The Panorama Landmarks are a response
to a competition by the East Anglian
Development Agency for a "Landmark for
the East of England." The projects define an
architectural landscape of local specificity as
well as providing a visual spectacle of both
panoramic and human proportions. The East
of England is a predominantly flat landscape.
The region has an intimacy with its climate
where the distant horizon and voluminous sky
have inspired artists and holidaymakers alike.

The landscape is observed as a panorama, a
circular gaze that encompasses the complete
horizon in one go. Each landmark seeks to
enhance this relationship between ground and
sky, utilizing elevated positions, constructed
vistas, and reflective surfaces. They reach out to
the sea and up to the clouds. The landmarks,

Self examination booklet of day shapes, signals,
and pyrotechnics that could be encountered at
sea under the *Collision Regulations, Notices to
Mariners and the Lateral System of Buoyage* used
in the United Kingdom

in addition to controlling or exploiting the
view from within, are experienced on or
in the landscape from remote positions.

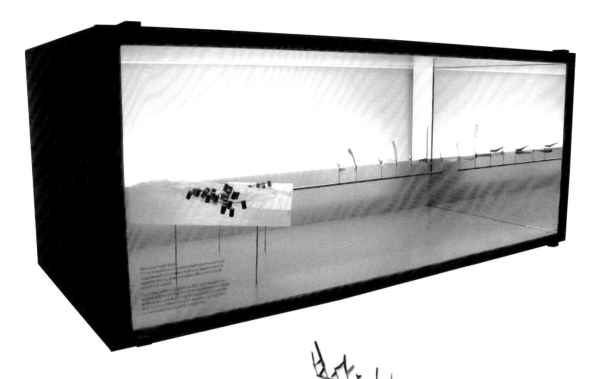

Dunes and Drifts

England's North Norfolk coast is a shifting landscape of sea and sand. Long shore drift and strong prevailing winds have shaped a region of expansive beaches, dunes, and crumbling cliffs—a landscape of currents and contours, sandbanks and quick sands, erosion and deposition.

The landmark inhabits a marginal territory with one foot on land and the other in the water. The shallow and fluctuating horizon of the sea is occupied by a string of "drift markers" that react to and demonstrate the motions of the sea and wind.

A top limb is designed to glint like white horses on the waves, while a lower limb acts as a rudder in the current.

The dunes are occupied by a net of tubs that become partially buried in the sand and reveal the endlessly shifting form of the dune landscape. Each tub marks out the transitory seasonal territory of the holidaymaker. The tubs are just big enough to accommodate paraphernalia for a day trip to the British seaside: a deck chair, cricket bat, picnic rug, and hut for shelter.

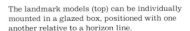

The landmark models (top) can be individually mounted in a glazed box, positioned with one another relative to a horizon line.

Deployable tents offer shelter from
the sun. The tents are printed with
thermochromic inks, which register
the degree of exposure to UV rays.

Individual dune tub with
deck chair / cricket bat, ball
and stumps / picnic rug / hut

Down   Up

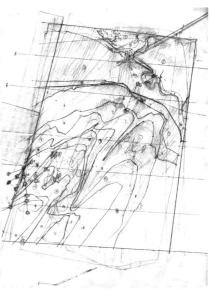

A Market in the Marshes

The estuaries of Essex form a liquid edge to the county. This fragile boundary, which extends and retracts with the ebb and flow of the tide, reinforces the connection between the sea and the land. The proposal responds to current thinking on a "managed realignment" of the coast, removing hard sea defenses such as sea walls and embankments that prevent the natural landward movement of the salt marshes, and allowing the land to be flooded by the incoming tide. Returning land to salt marsh encourages brackish vegetation and establishes the flood plain as an environmental buffer. A shallow plate is inserted into the intertidal zone, lying low on the horizon. The plate beds into the mud flats, with its extremities in the retreating tide and reaching up to the higher grass land beyond.

Diagrammatic section: At twilight clouds of moths form a shimmering halo to the market platform. The moths are attracted to the oyster farm's UV treatment baths. Reflective panels that accentuate the extended horizon of the marsh bring a continuous "skyscape" into the market.

Three territories are formed: oyster lanes fed by nutrient-rich runoff from the salt marsh and high tide, grazing land, and a market. The panorama is framed and partially concealed by a tilted reflective edge to the marketplace, which reaches out endlessly between the sea and sky.

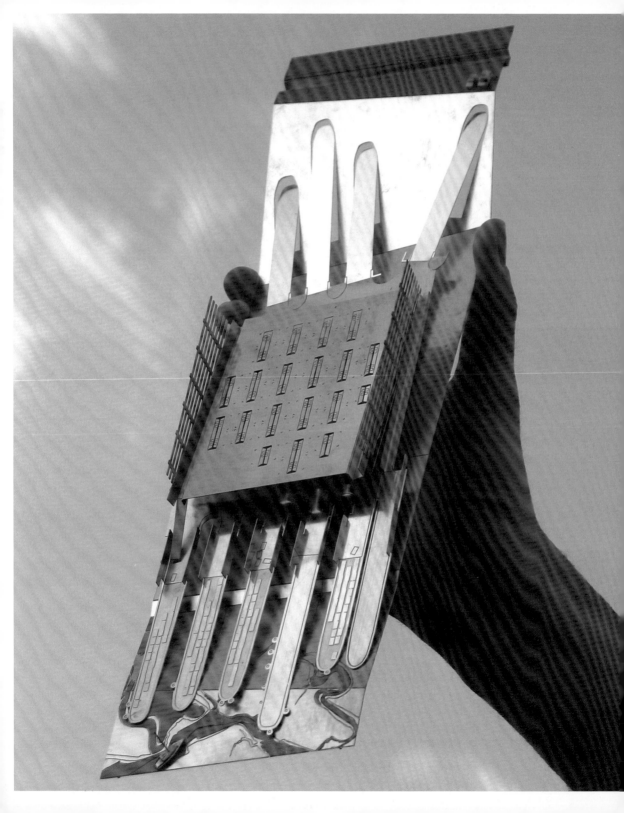

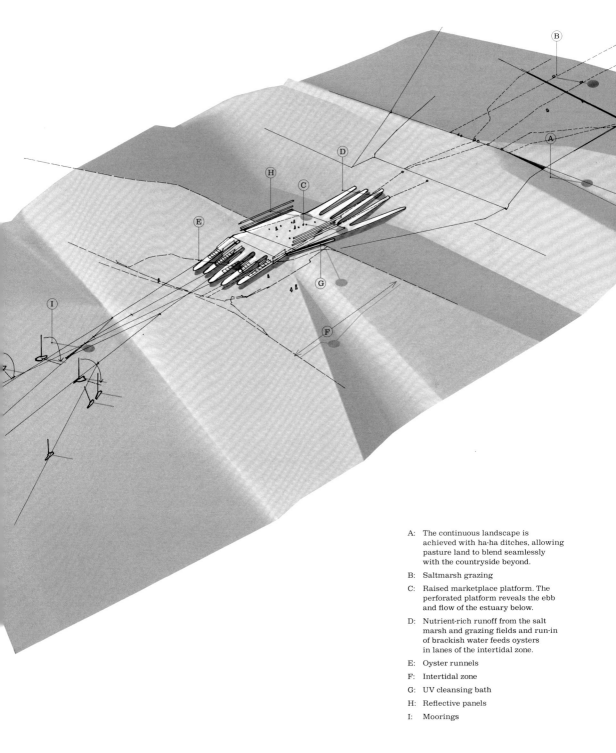

A: The continuous landscape is
   achieved with ha-ha ditches, allowing
   pasture land to blend seamlessly
   with the countryside beyond.

B: Saltmarsh grazing

C: Raised marketplace platform. The
   perforated platform reveals the ebb
   and flow of the estuary below.

D: Nutrient-rich runoff from the salt
   marsh and grazing fields and run-in
   of brackish water feeds oysters
   in lanes of the intertidal zone.

E: Oyster runnels

F: Intertidal zone

G: UV cleansing bath

H: Reflective panels

I: Moorings

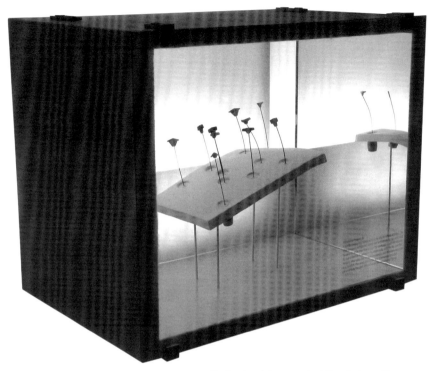

The Landmark boxes are backlit and mirrored to indicate the panoramic gaze, reflected skies, and the repetition of elements of the design.

Dunstable Downs Kite Farm

The chalk escarpment and gently rolling topography of Bedfordshire's Dunstable Downs create thermal currents that rise from the plain attracting numerous aeronautical enthusiasts to the region. This is the site for a flock of wind "kites." Each kite records its movement as it swoops—its relationship with the sky and the horizon.

The kites occupy a vertiginous space, the territory of the sky, reacting to currents of air flowing across the landscape. Each one is connected to the ground by a flexible pole. They are anchored to a pivoting base that is mounted in a water-filled reservoir to limit and slow movement. A pair of cameras mounted on each kite relays stereoscopic live images to the pilot's viewpoint, providing a three-dimensional panorama from the perspective of the kite. As the horizon appears to hover and glide, the pilot achieves the sensation of flying.

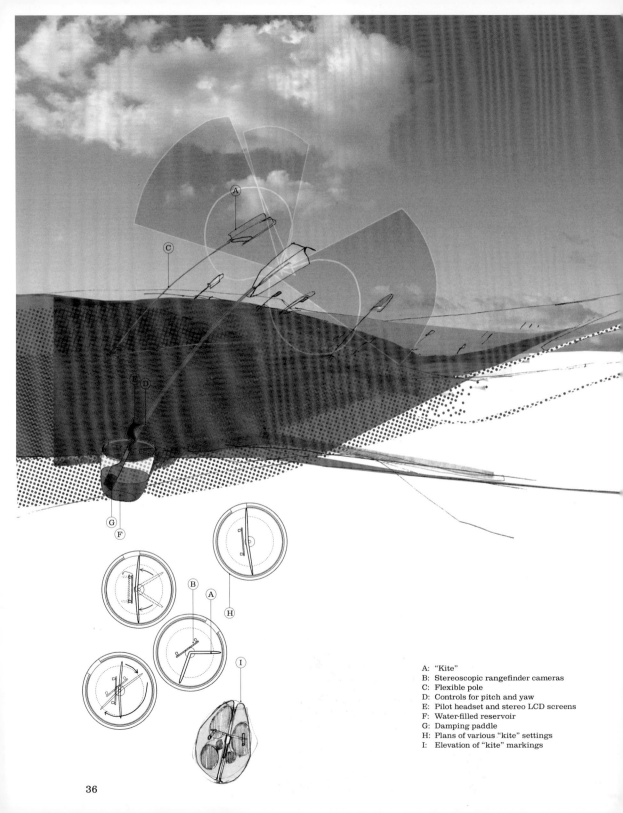

A: "Kite"
B: Stereoscopic rangefinder cameras
C: Flexible pole
D: Controls for pitch and yaw
E: Pilot headset and stereo LCD screens
F: Water-filled reservoir
G: Damping paddle
H: Plans of various "kite" settings
I: Elevation of "kite" markings

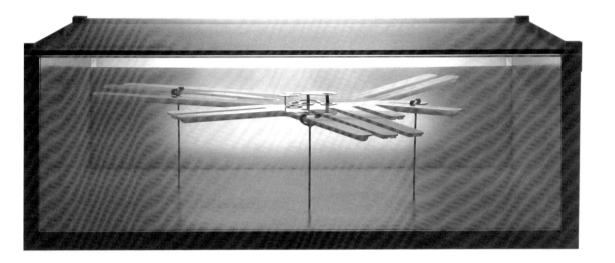

Fenland Obscura

The fen landscape is governed by the straight lines of man-made marks across the flat plain. Roads, railways, and rivers run parallel and perpendicular to each other, often raised above the ground level. Drainage ditches and dykes that cut into the black ground at regular intervals demarcate field boundaries. The Fenland Obscura landmark echoes this pattern of levees and drains, replacing them with bathing water, ponds, and iced surfaces. It also acknowledges the growth of scientific industries in the region, utilizing sustainable environmental technologies to enhance the nature of the site. A central platform houses a camera obscura which observes both the array of channels and the landscape beyond. The obscura digitally projects the panoramic image to a table that is enabled with interactive gesture-recognition software. When touched, the image is annotated with contextual information such as geography, geology, meteorology, history, or commerce. In addition, a touch of the image selects a hue, the wall of the obscura room is washed with light—a spectrum of ever-changing hues.

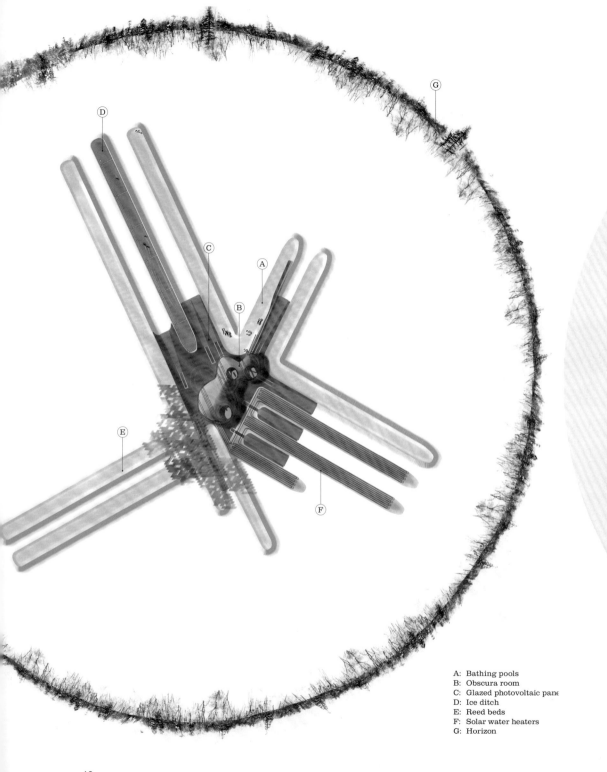

A: Bathing pools
B: Obscura room
C: Glazed photovoltaic pane
D: Ice ditch
E: Reed beds
F: Solar water heaters
G: Horizon

Enhancing the physical with the digital: The camera obscura receives a 360° view of the landmark and its landscape. Its reflective surface of glass, ice, and water appear as a mirror to the sky. This is particularly apparent when looking through the camera obscura from above.

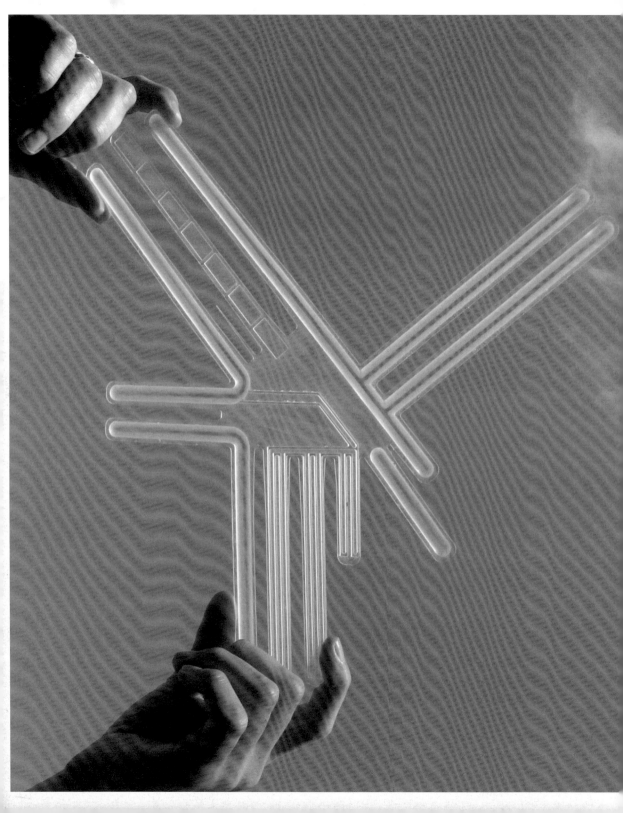

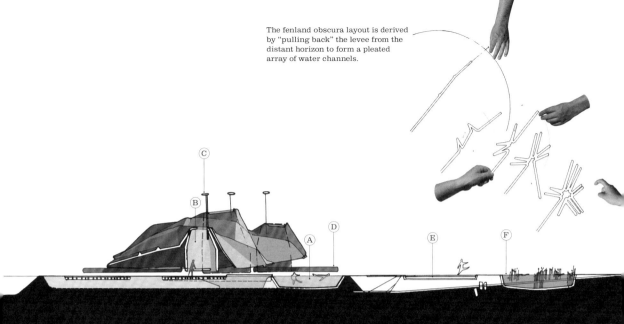

The fenland obscura layout is derived by "pulling back" the levee from the distant horizon to form a pleated array of water channels.

A: Bathing pools
   Solar water heaters provide a continual flow of warm water.

B: Obscura room

C: Digital camera obscura masts

D: Glazed photovoltaic panels make up a raised platform on which the obscura room sits.

E: Ice ditch
   Twice daily, an iced surface is quickly created by the release of compressed gas through metal plates beneath the surface of the water. The compressor is powered by a raised central platform surface of photovoltaic cells [D]. 450m² of photovoltaic panels power the gas compressor. Excess energy is returned to national grid.

   To freeze the ice ditch in 20 minutes:

   Assuming ditch is 70m x 6m x 10mm, 1kW from 1m² of cell and temperature gradient is 15°C.

   Mass of H_2O x Temp Change x Specific Heat Capacity of H_2O = Joules

   4200000g x 15 x 4.2 = 264,600,000J

   Joules/Seconds = Watts

   264,600,600/1200 = 220kW

   assuming 50% efficency of process

   440kW = 440m² of cell

F: Reed beds continually provide clean water for the bathing pools.

Inhabiting the Horizon and Shape Recognition:
Where Things Fly Up and Outward

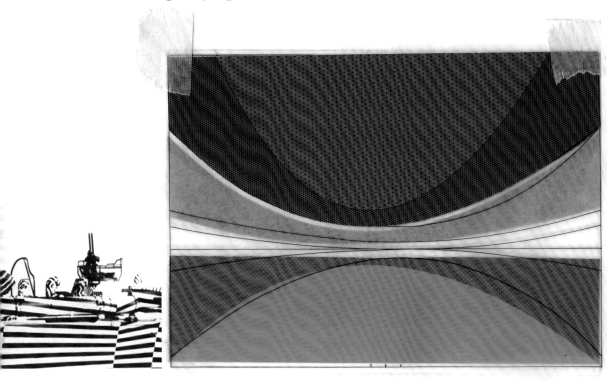

In a flat landscape the horizon, where sky and land meet, is an indeterminably deep boundary. Distance is accentuated, and the mid- and fore-grounds blend together. The horizon line, although observable seems an uninhabitable margin—objects here are fixed onto rather than into this depth of space. Its appearance is mutable, daily and seasonal fluctuations of light modify the colour and contrast of the sky and that of the objects that it touches.

A series of ballistic instruments are designed to momentarily occupy the space between the sky and the ground. Camouflage strategies employed by nature and in the design of disruptive pattern materials to conceal an

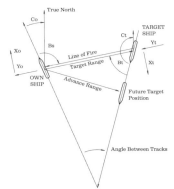

Co Own ship's course
So Own ship's speed
Xo Component of own ship's speed normal to line of fire
Yo Component of own ship's speed along line of fire
Ct Target's course
St Target's speed
Xt Component of target ship's speed normal to line of fire
Yt Component of target ship's speed along line of fire
Bt Target angle (target's course w/ respect to line of fire)
Bs Relative target bearing

Measurement angles for targeting the position and trajectory of a moving object on the horizon.

"Beyond the horizon lies the unknown, that
which we do not see... the voyages of the
renaissance and all subsequent endeavors have
eroded the primitive and perhaps essential
relationship of humankind to nature; for now
instead of being comfortably enclosed in the
vault of the sky with its limit at the horizon,
we are alone in infinite space." —Sverre Fehn

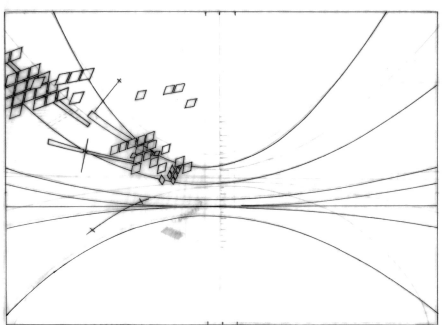

object within its environment can in much the same way be designed to accentuate and reveal figure and position. The instruments use shape, shine, shadow, and silhouette to enable visual recognition of form and consequently to examine the apparent depth of the horizon. Their performance adds to both our objective knowledge of the space and to our subjective experience. The ballistic devices are launched into the sky, propelled up and outward with considerable accuracy. Each deploys at a given height and speed. A split-second spatial event is triggered which reveals the nature of the sites which they temporarily occupy.

"Gestalt" theory examines the organization of perception and considers the observation that the perception of the whole is different from the sum of the parts: When seeing, the viewer perceives a unified form, the whole, rather than reading the individual and independent fragments within the form. This theory can be used to predict how a viewer will read and respond to an image.

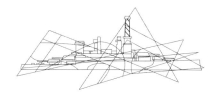

A: Weighted cap is released to
   allow the net to be cast
B: Woven net and reflective nodes
C: The non-reflective body disappears
   into the background during flight
D: Stabilizing fins
E: Drogue parachutes

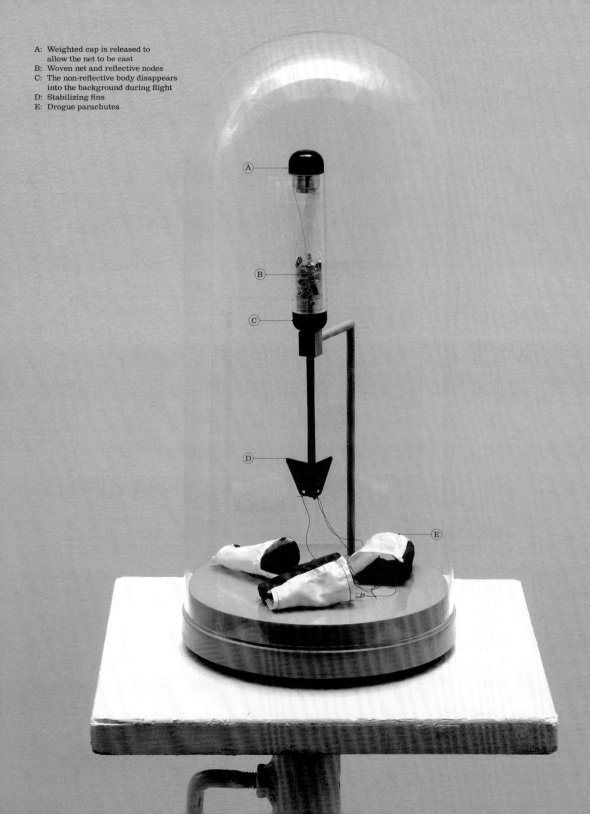

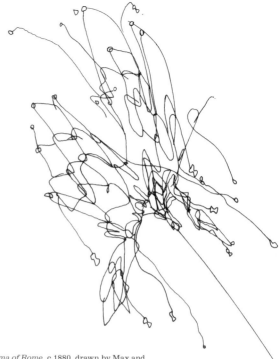

Diorama of Rome, c.1880, drawn by Max and Gotthold Brückner is variably backlit to simulate natural light conditions at dawn and dusk for theatrical effect.

A "net" of reflective pieces infiltrates the depth of the blurred or fractured horizon to reveal silhouettes as deep three-dimensional objects.

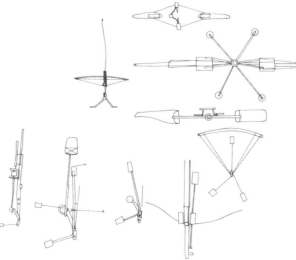

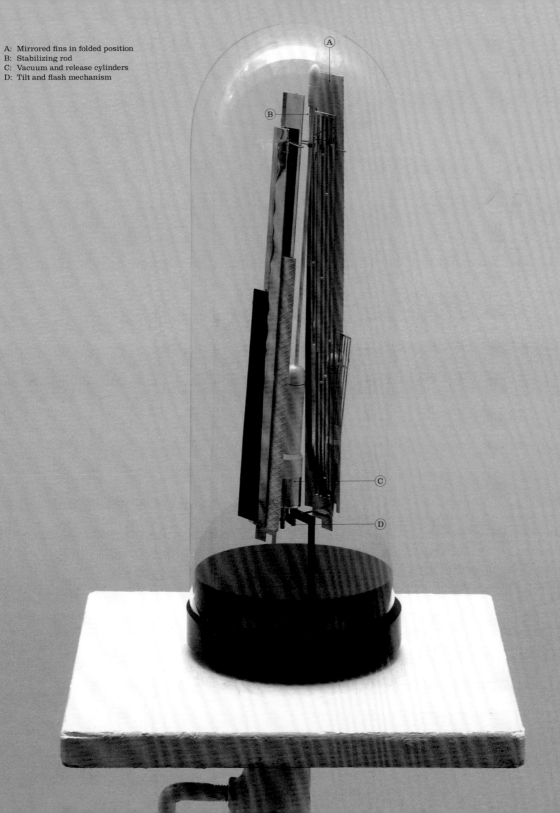

A: Mirrored fins in folded position
B: Stabilizing rod
C: Vacuum and release cylinders
D: Tilt and flash mechanism

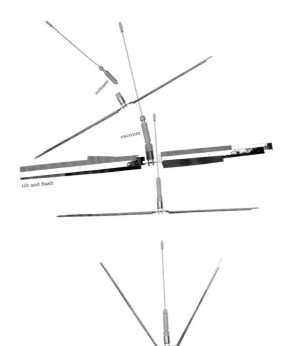

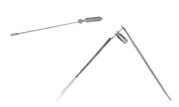

The "glint" instrument illuminates the distance of the horizon, momentarily foreshortening the three-dimensional space between foreground and background. Whilst in midair (right), mirrored fins are opened out and, for an instant, are tilted to flash to the observer. Varying intensities of reflectance are produced depending on the triangulation of the fins, the viewer and, the light source.

A reference for these studies is the work of Caspar David Freidrich, whose paintings, which intimately observed the richness of nature in delicate colour harmonies, construct landscapes through impossible geometries. *The Great Preserve*, 1832.

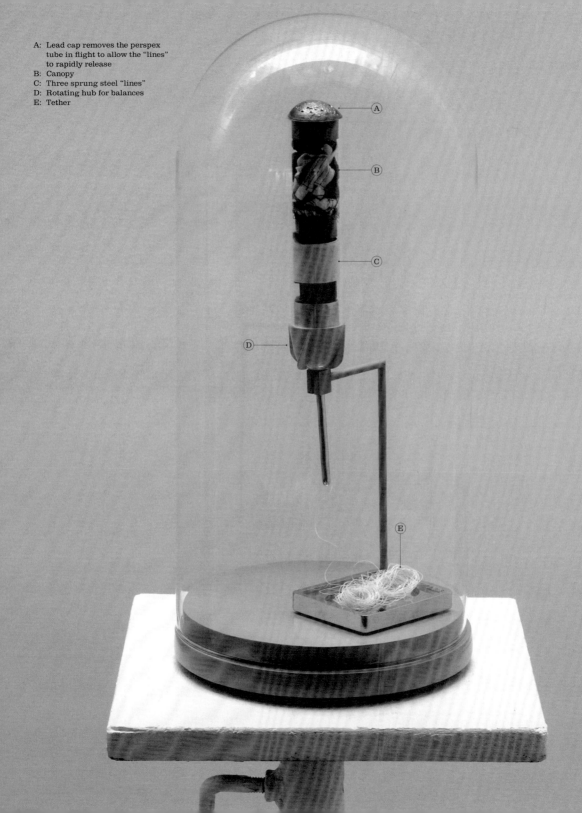

A: Lead cap removes the perspex tube in flight to allow the "lines" to rapidly release
B: Canopy
C: Three sprung steel "lines"
D: Rotating hub for balances
E: Tether

The third instrument is specifically deployed in an urban environment where one is more intimately surrounded by an irregular and interrupted horizon. The instrument employs a "dynamic line" that rapidly unravels in flight. A line is literally drawn along the hard edge of the occupied sky.

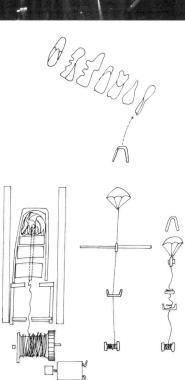

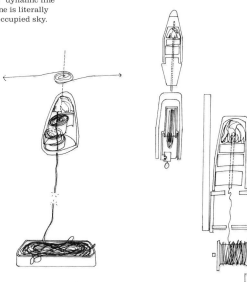

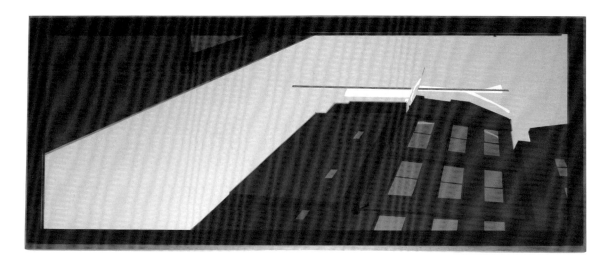

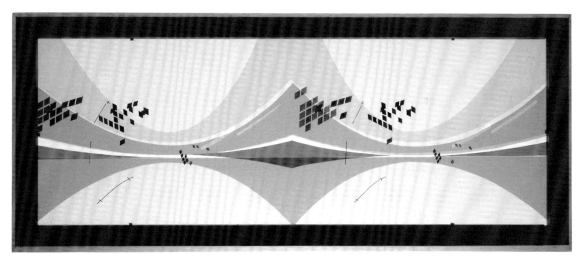

The ballistic devices are observed and empirically read to inform strategies for architectural concealment and revelation. Their performance and landscape is interpreted in three assemblages of light, metal, and colored film. Each painting is backlit generating a balance of projected and reflected light, subtle gradients of color are thus revealed in the apparently flat black silhouettes.

Light-Box Paintings: (opposite) *The Net* in which silver wire is encapsulated between etched brass tree silhouettes, (top) *The Dynamic Line*, (bottom) *The Glint Assemblage* in which stereoscopic views place the spatial event in a deep three-dimensional space.

53

The Retreating Village:
Architecture for a Restless Landscape

The coastal village of Happisburgh in North Norfolk is falling into the sea. The cliffs, dunes, and sea defense structures that protect this predominately low-lying county and its extensive freshwater Broads from inundation cannot contend with the force of rising sea levels and climate change. Government policies that "allow coastal retreat through no active intervention,"[5] such as the Shoreline Management Plans, have conspired to leave the village undefended from the action of the sea and the wind. Streets, hotels, houses, sheds, and flower beds which had always been perilously close to the cliff, have all gone over the edge.

The fifteen mile stretch of coast from Cromer to Happisburgh is the most actively eroding stretch of Norfolk coastline. There is evidence that hard sea defences such as concrete sea walls, wooden revetments, and groynes, although providing protection for the immediate beach and cliff, magnify problems elsewhere. Allowed to erode naturally, they supply sediment for beaches further along the coast, and these beaches safeguard other villages and towns. A natural deep beach provides protection against the waves until the cliff and beach reach a sustainable position. Further along the coast defenses are provided and maintained where the local council deems them justifiable. However, there is a long-term view to retreat and relocate.

The retreating village is a sustainable settlement that responds to the changing conditions of the landscape. This is nothing new. T. Rowley and J. Wood, in their publication *Deserted Villages*, suggest that "Settlements are organic and constantly changing. Villages have prospered, declined and migrated to new sites for a wide variety of social, cultural and economic reasons as they have responded to changing conditions."[6] When read from the air the landscape provides evidence of the deserted villages. Former buildings and paths leave banks and hollows in the ground as markings of their layout and land use.

Our proposal for a retreating village of small houses and streets is deployed in the disintegrating territory between the sea and the land. The village reacts to predicted rates of retreat, as much as five meters per year, by sliding and shifting to safer land. To achieve this the scheme employs a mechanical landscape of winches, pulleys, rails, and counterweights, mimicking techniques for hauling boats from the waves. It also adopts an architectural language of impermanence, of permeable screens, loose-fit structures, and cheap materials that complement and contribute to the nature of the restless landscape.

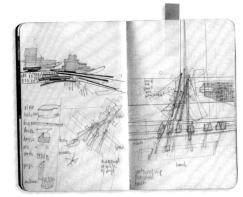

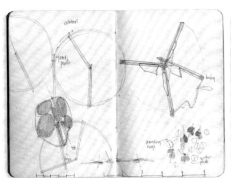
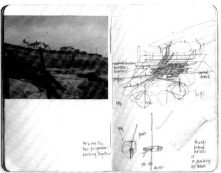
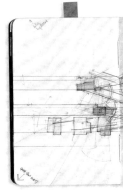

The architecture responds to its position, sited on a shifting and elevated horizon. The main inhabitable spaces are concealed behind large slatted revetments that provide secondary protection from the elements. The slats are reflective on one side and are tilted and placed eccentrically to achieve a disruptive pattern. The pattern, which aims to disguise the village on the cliff and to make its elevation and location less tangible, adds to the sense of the site and the architecture losing ground to the sea. The proposal is examined and designed through an ongoing series of working drawings, existing between the territories of sketch diagrams and architectural orthographic representations. They contain multiple viewpoints and simultaneous dynamic shifts of position.

The village is shown, suspended in a twitchy attitude, in its inevitable withdrawal from the edge. The architecture and the landscape are marked by this continual performance.

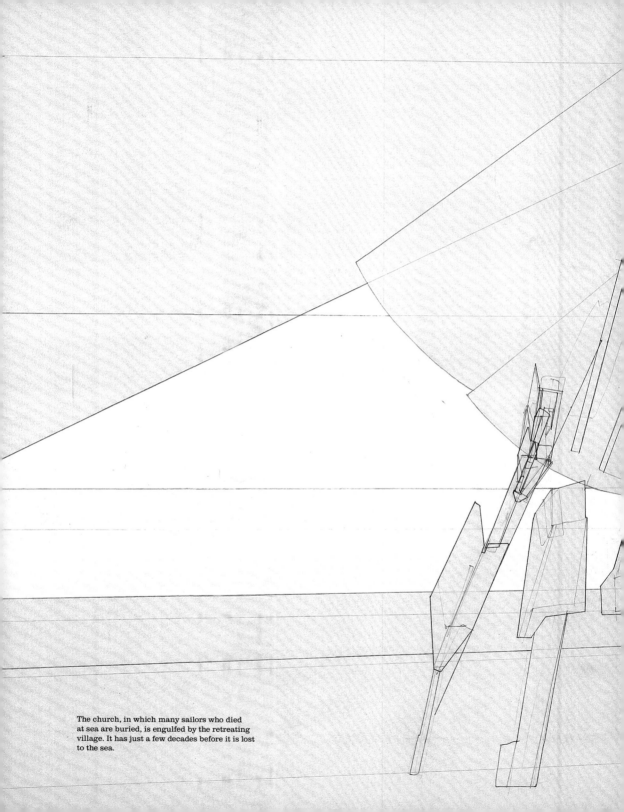

The church, in which many sailors who died
at sea are buried, is engulfed by the retreating
village. It has just a few decades before it is lost
to the sea.

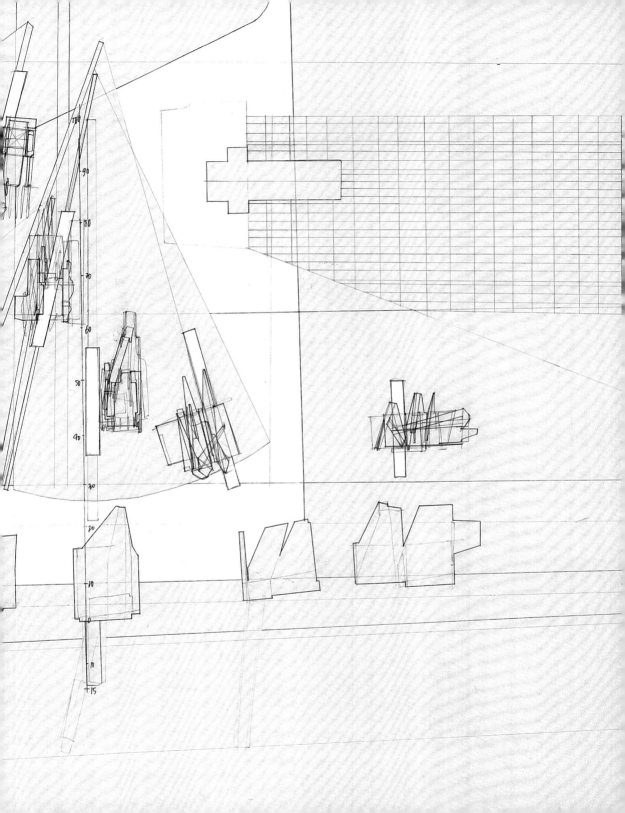

Cliff elevation. The village is constructed of
revetment structures that are larger and more
articulated than the hulk enclosures they
conceal. Staircases, ramps and ladders infiltrate
the disruptive pattern of the facades.

0

-1

-2

Beams, arcs, and matresses dominate the
landscape. Remnants remain of footings and
paths that evoke the past life of the village.

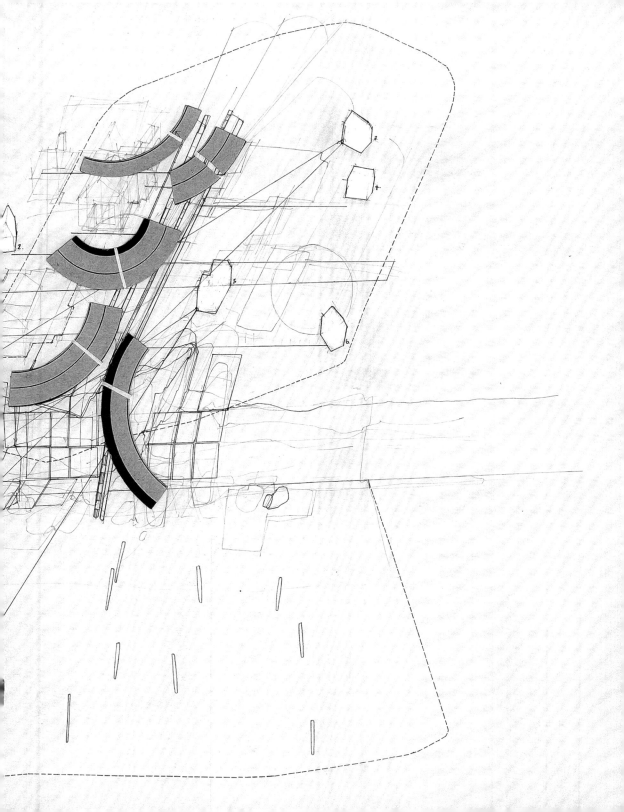

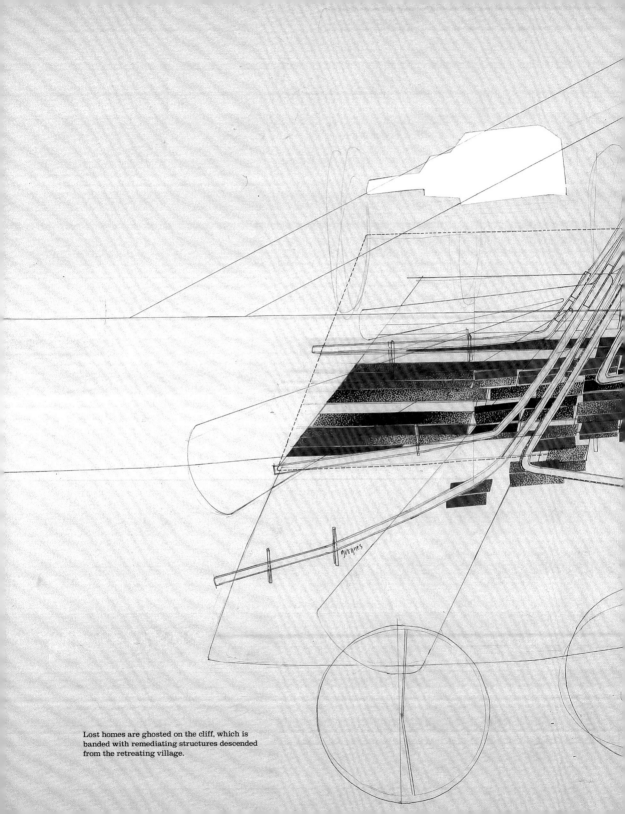

Lost homes are ghosted on the cliff, which is
banded with remediating structures descended
from the retreating village.

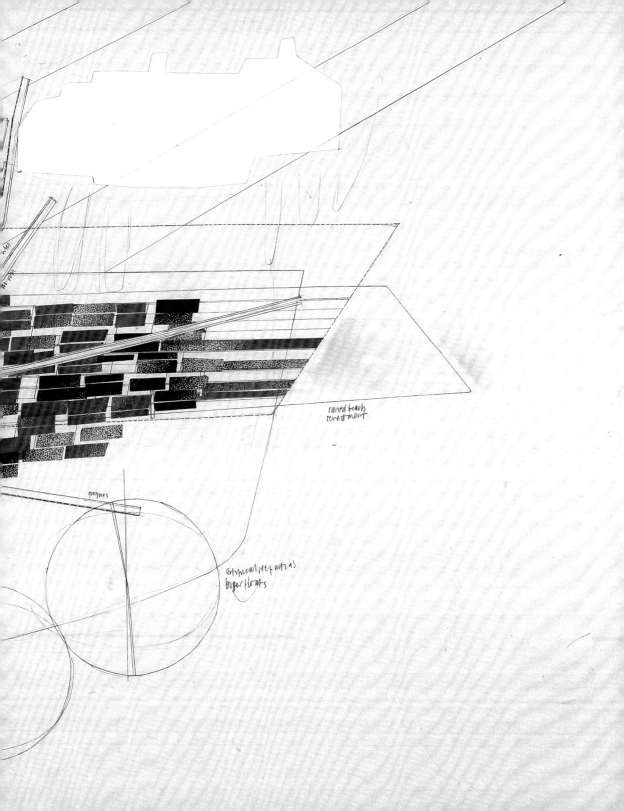

raised beach
revetment

groynes

artificial reef acts as
super floats

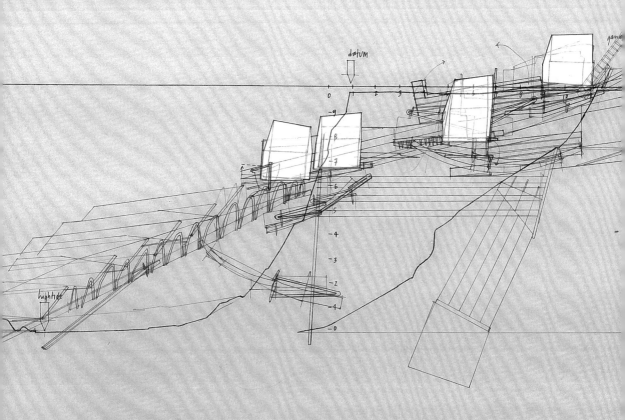

datum

0 1 2 3

−9

−8

−7

−6

−5

−4

−3

−2

−1

−0

highfide

gann

Cliff section showing repositioning and
reconfiguration.

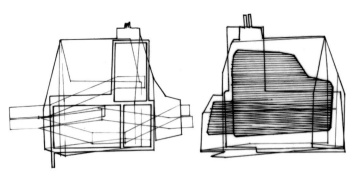

Hulk:
Each house occupies the silhouette of a lost property. The new house takes the form of a "hulk" or solid enclosure inside which most of the house's normal functions are placed. Revetment shutters appear to protect the hulk and its occupants from the weather. However, access ramps and ladder staircases puncture between the skins. The houses literally fold up or stretch out in their changing hinterland.

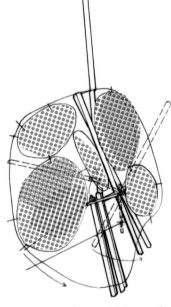

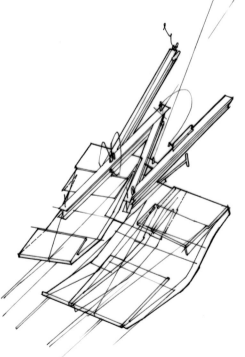

Faggots:
Bioengineering approaches for coastal defense are low-impact retaining techniques that retard erosion. Coir rolls, or "soft" revetments of planted nets, simultaneously control erosion and provide a natural habitat. In areas of more aggressive erosion they can be combined with faggots and fascines, made from live cuttings of hazel, chestnut, or willow bundles that provide the support for the coir rolls. The cuttings sprout and, as roots secure the soil, they become a living and sustainable revetment.

Beams and Arcs:
The village is slipped, dragged, and rotated by a mechanism of anchors, ground beams, and concreted arcs.

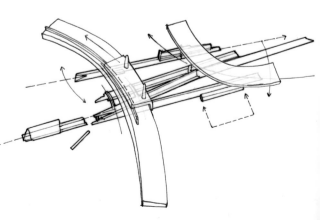

Skids:
The village is mounted on steel and concrete skids that allow each house to be dragged across the landscape. They are manipulated by no fewer than three pulleys that are anchored in the landscape and attached to the frame mounted above the skids and below the floor of the house.

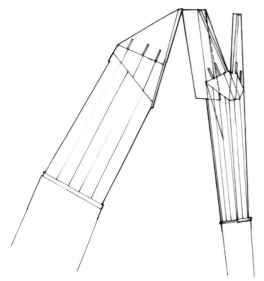

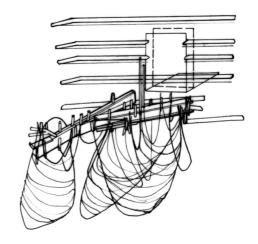

Props:
Temporary timber props strengthen the cliff in critical areas until they are eventually engulfed by the landscape.

Gardens:
Each house travels with a "garden" of rope that reinforces the surrounding soil. These three-dimensionally woven geotextile bags are connected to frames and fed out through "windows" in the revetments. For some villagers the baskets and rope gardens are used as allotments for prize-winning vegetables; for others they provide a personal space for sunbathing.

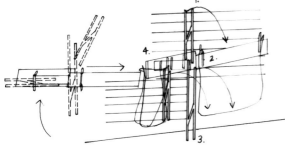

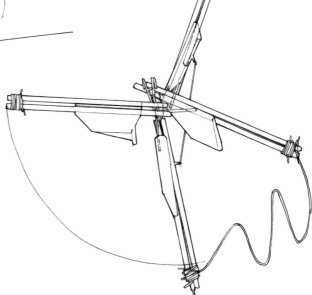

Frame:
The rope gardens are fed out on a counterbalanced ratchet whose equilibrium is interrupted by the movement of the village and the cliff edge.

Buoys:
The sea is populated by a swarm of floats that are flexible and dynamic to allow them to be reconfigured by the waves. The buoys act as beacons for the village to warn of inclement weather.

A 1:200 model of the village shows two houses, a strip of cliff, arcs, beams, rope gardens, and the paraphernalia of haulage set in a circular case. The village is rotated and viewed at eye level through breaks in the horizon which is marked against the back wall.

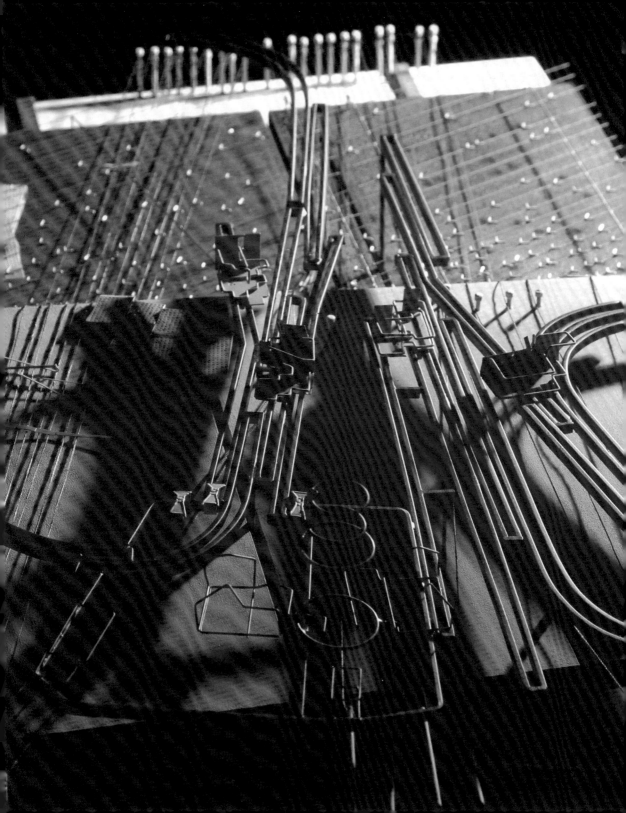

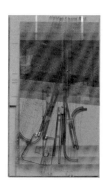

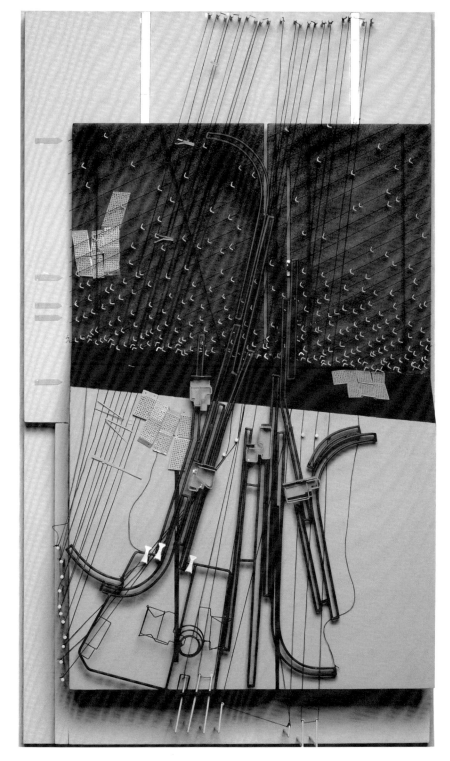

A 1:500 model shows the traces and
trajectory of the village locked onto
a frame on the cliff top. The action of
the waves and faggots that reinforce
the edge appear as the cliff recedes.

Acknowledgments

We dedicate this publication to Ellis, our beautiful baby.

We thank our family and friends for their support during the production of this book and the projects shown here. We thank Iain Borden, Stephen Gage, Jane Rendell, and Neil Spiller at the Bartlett School of Architecture, UCL, and Peter Cook for their continued inspiration and encouragement. Abi Abdolwahabi, Bim Burton, Richard Grimes, Asif Khan, Poppy Kirkwood, Ian Lawrence, Karl Normanton, Luke Pearson, Aaron Lim, Ben Ridley, Gavin Robotham, and Rion Willard have all provided much needed assistance. Additional hands supplied by Emma Kirkman, Ian Lawrence, and Aaron Lim. Grand Egyptian Musem, Giza, initial design in collaboration with Gavin Robotham. We thank Richard Stonehouse for his suberb photography, pp. 15, 18, 46, 48, 50, 52–53, 74–77, 79.

The research projects shown here are supported by both The Bartlett School of Architecture Research Fund and the Graduate School Research Fund, UCL.

Image Credits

p. 6, Onokami Village, courtesy of Toshio Shibata, Landscape, Nazraeli Press. p. 6, *Oxford Tire Pile #8, Westley, California*, Edward Burtynsky; courtesy of Charles Cowles Gallery, New York; Robert Koch Gallery, San Francisco; Nicholas Metivier Gallery, Toronto. p. 7, Dauphin Island, courtesy of The Center for Land Use Interpretation. p. 8, Claude Glass, courtesy of V&A Images, The Victoria & Albert Museum. p. 9, *Annie Get Your Gun*, courtesy of Paul Davis. p.17, Isfahan Nesf-e Jahan, courtesy of Dr. Ataollah Omidvar. p. 34, Front Coming In, courtesy of Neil Wykes. p. 38, Vermuydens' Drain, courtesy of Lizanne Ford. p. 44, NYP13306, courtesy of the Imperial War Museum, London.

Notes

[1] Stephan Oettermann, *The Panorama History of a Mass Medium* (New York: Urzone,1997).
[2] Jørgen Dehs, "Sense of Landscape: Reflections on a Concept, a Metaphor, a Model," in *Essays on Space and Science*, ed. Peter Weibel (Graz, Austria, and Cambridge, MA: Neue Gallery and MIT Press, 2000), 166–75.
[3] Susan Stewart, *On Longing: Narratives of the Miniature, the Gigantic, the Souvenir, the Collection* (Durham, NC: Duke University Press, USA, 1999), 71.
[4] Richard Mabey, *Nature Cure* (London: Pimlico, 2006).
[5] Anglian Coastal Authorities Group, "Kelling to Lowestoft Ness Shoreline Management Plan, Policy Unit 3b12: Ostend to Eccles," http://www.northnorfolk.org/acag/default_smp.ht, 2005.
[6] T. Rowley & J. Wood, *Deserted Villages* (Buckinghamshire: Shire Publications, 1995).

Pamphlet Architecture was initiated in 1977 as an independent vehicle to criticize, question, and exchange views. Each issue is assembled by an individual author/architect.

For more information, Pamphlet proposals, or contributions, please write to: Pamphlet Architecture, c/o Princeton Architectural Press, 37 E. 7th Street, New York, NY 10003, or go to http://www.pamphletarchitecture.org.

Pamphlets Published:

1. Bridges	S. Holl	1977*
2. 10 California Houses	M. Mack	1978*
3. Villa Prima Facie	L. Lerup	1978*
4. Stairwells	L. Dimitriu	1979*
5.The Alphabetical City	S. Holl	1980
6. Einstein Tomb	L. Woods	1980*
7. Bridge of Houses	S. Holl	1981*
8. Planetary Architecture	Z. Hadid	1981*
9. Rural and Urban House Types	S. Holl	1981*
10. Metafisca Della Architectura	A. Sartoris	1984*
11. Hybrid Buildings	J. Fenton	1985
12. Building; Machines	R. McCarter	1987
13. Edge of a City	S. Holl	1991
14. Mosquitos	K. Kaplan, T. Krueger	1993
15. War and Architecture	L. Woods	1993
16. Architecture as a Translation of Music	E. Martin	1994
17. Small Buildings	M. Caldwell	1996
19. Reading Drawing Building	M. Silver	1996
20. Seven Partly Underground Rooms	M. A. Ray	1997
21. Situation Normal…	Lewis.Tsurumaki.Lewis	1998
22. Other Plans	Michael Sorkin Studio	2001
23. Move	J. S. Dickson	2002
24. Some Among Them are Killers	D. Ross	2003
25. Gravity	J. Cathcart et al.	2003
26. 13 Projects for the Sheridan Expressway	J. Solomon	2004
27. Tooling	Aranda/Lasch	2006

*out of print, available only in the collection Pamphlet Architecture 1–10.